YOUR ROAD TO SELF-DISCOVERY AND LIFE RECOVERY

A PERSONAL GROWTH AND DEVELOPMENT SELF-HELP GUIDE WORKBOOK AND JOURNAL

CRYSTAL SCOTT, LMFT, M.A., B.S.

authorHOUSE

AuthorHouse™
1663 Liberty Drive
Bloomington, IN 47403
www.authorhouse.com
Phone: 1 (800) 839-8640

Published by AuthorHouse 10/16/2019

ISBN: 978-1-7283-3157-7 (sc)
ISBN: 978-1-7283-3156-0 (e)

Print information available on the last page.

CONTENTS

UNDERSTANDING YOUR SELF-HELP GUIDE AND HOW TO USE IT EFFECTIVELY

Your road to self-discovery and life discovery is a guide designed specifically and uniquely to fit your needs related to personal growth and development. This self-help guide is equipped with knowledge and tools you need to carve out and craft a life you will be satisfied with, and one you can enjoy.

I caution you to not compare yourself to others, you will do well to focus on your unique needs and allow the process to lead you to your desired goals. Sometimes it is difficult for some people to take slowly paced steps, but if you do not; information might not settle in as needed. You will gain information but if you move too quickly, pertinent information and insights might not take root.

Personal growth and development are like a marathon, not a sprint. For this reason, a journal section has been added to this workbook to help you keep your learning tools all in one place and keep your thoughts organized.

As you immerse yourself in this information, take your time and be very patient with yourself. Change takes place over time, but do know this; you are bound to change as you desire. Just be sure that you do not abandon your course. Stay on the road, keep your eyes peeled and your ears open, stay in your lane and you will enjoy the journey. All the best to you!

Sincerely,

Crystal Scott

REFRAME YOUR EXPERIENCES FOR A BETTER MENTAL AND EMOTIONAL PICTURE

The outer area is the frame containing your thoughts, emotions and responses.

THOUGHTS

EMOTIONS

RESPONSES

With this exercise, keep a daily log of your thoughts, emotions, and responses. Notice how certain days impact these three areas. For example, on days when you have experienced a good night's sleep; you might notice you can cope a little better as opposed to days when you did not get good sleep. Also, when your day's agenda is full and you are rushed and hurried; you are more likely to experience challenges to experiencing healthy thoughts, emotions, and behavioral responses. Don't be hard on yourself if you discover you are not responding as you would like to. Remember, you are in the process of recovering your life and doing the work to become a better functioning you.

THOUGHTS	EMOTIONS	RESPONSES

Activity 2

PICTURE THIS

In this exercise, each frame represents your mind, and the numbers represent the measurement of your thought processes. As you have learned new insights over the years, the size of your frame enlarges. Perhaps you were once a wallet size thinker, but now you have matured and developed into a greater mindset of a 7 X 9 thinker. If you try to revert back to wallet size thinking you will not fit into that old frame. Your thinking has enlarged. Therefore, to fit back into a smaller frame you would have to reduce your thinking and mentality.

Make an agreement with yourself that you will not allow yourself to be cut down to a smaller size in your thought processes. Don't dummy down what you have accomplished by way of personal growth and development. You have grown and you have learned a lot; if you try to revert back to your old thought processes, you will not be a happy person. You already know too much and you have come such a long way. Stick with your course and stay on the road to life recovery.

As you review the frames on the next page, take a moment to reflect and assess where you are in your thinking today. Allow these frames to serve as a mental imagery and reminder of your progress. In the journal section of this workbook, jot down your thoughts. You might be surprised that you have gained more insights than you have given yourself credit for.

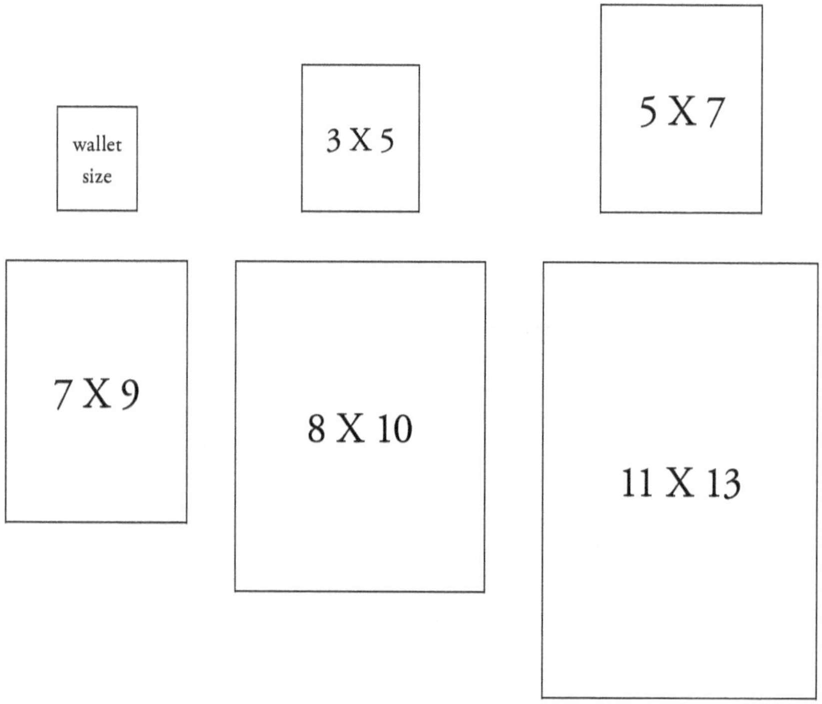

wallet
size
3 X 5
5 X 7
7 X 9
8 X 10
11 X 13

THOUGHTFULNESS AND LIFE MANAGEMENT EXERCISE

I woke up one morning and enjoyed a wonderful empowering experience I would like to share with you. I decided to remain in bed a moment before arising to begin my day. Initially, I thought of how grateful I was to be alive, and then I focused on the many blessings I sometimes do not give enough attention to and express gratitude for. I began to express thankfulness for being able to walk on my own and take care of my basic daily needs, as well as my hygiene, and ability to take care of responsibilities included in managing and maintaining my personal and business needs.

Then I experienced more thoughts of how I can incorporate my gratitude into something that might be helpful to you. I created a helpful exercise for myself that would remind me of the importance of slowing down my thoughts and actions in the morning, and getting in touch with the power of my mind. So, while still in bed, I closed my eyes. I imagined my room as empty of everything except me and my bed, and my room represented my day. I then decided that I get to fill my room with whatever I desire that I would include on my daily agenda.

Here is your challenge. Think of things you are grateful or appreciative for and go to back of this workbook and include them in your journal entry for today. Now come back to this exercise. Each square represents a day of the week. Begin to write in today's square, what you intend to accomplish. Try to adorn your room with things to do that are only necessary for today. Have fun with this. Arrange your thoughts with words or feel free to use cut out images from a magazine. As much as possible, add something in your room that allows room for you to engage in me-time.

DAY 1

Day 2

Day 3

Day 4

Day 5

DAY 6

DAY 7

MIND MATTERS

Using the same day blocks in the previous exercise, I want you to consider the squares as a symbolism of your mind. You awaken and with your eyes closed, you empty your image of your room. Only you and your bed are there. With your room as a symbolism of your mind, decide what thoughts and emotions you will fill your room with today.

ACTIVITY 4

COMMUNICATION AND WELLNESS BINGO

What type of communicator are you? Whether facially, bodily, or verbally; you are communicating all the time. Write your name on the blank line. Feel free to have fun with this bingo exercise and share with others. If you are able to get four in a row, reward yourself. If you do not get four in a row; work on the areas of your struggle and pretty soon you will completely bingo out. For more information on how to be a more effective communicator, I refer you to my book: Communication and You.

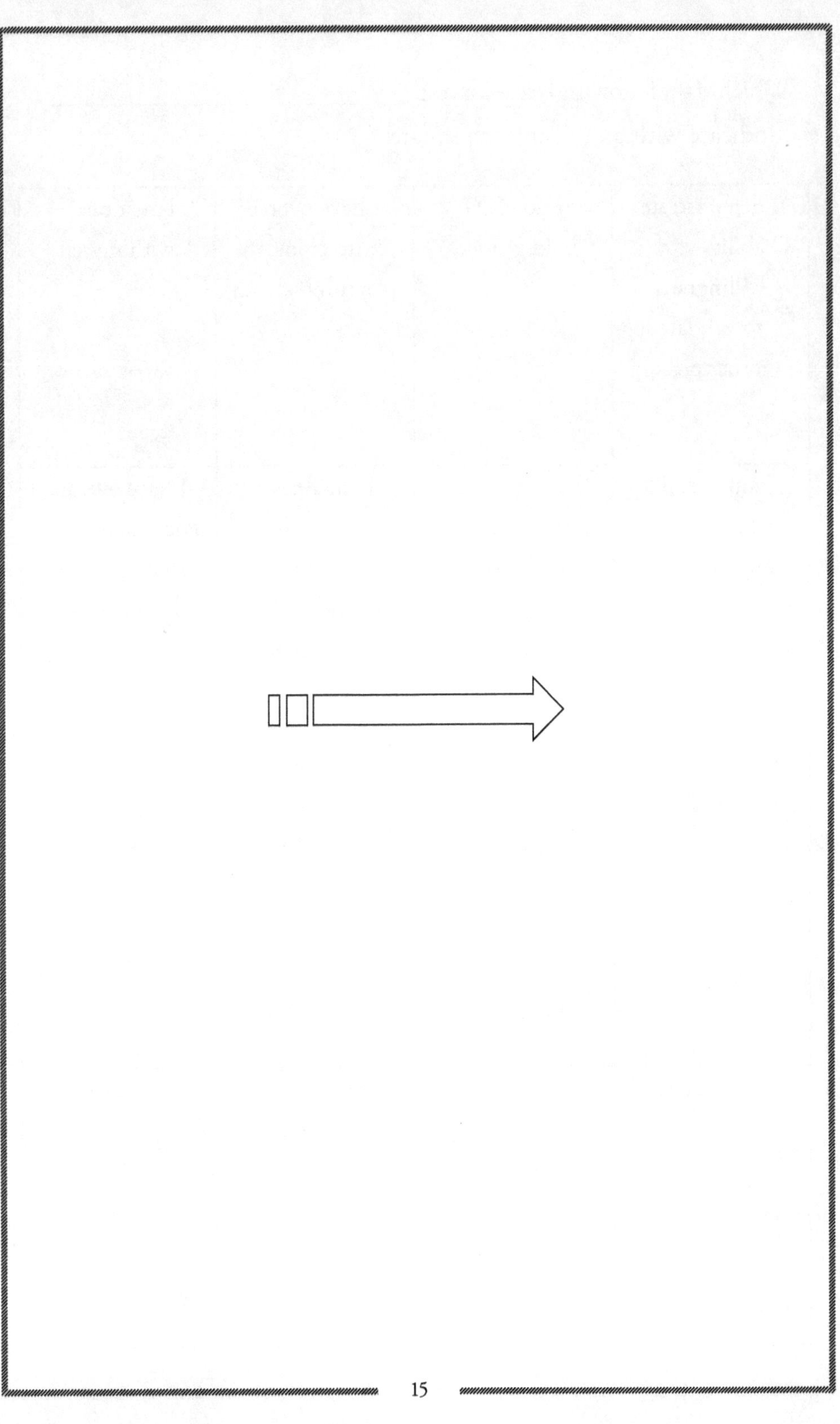

Which of the following is true for you?_______________________________
. Indicate with an (X) in each square.

I demonstrate ability and willingness to validate another person	I do NOT hold grudges	I have people to enjoy playfulness with	I'm at peace with myself
I am overall, achieving life and work goals	I am quick to resolve conflict effectively	I am able to accept when other people provide positive acknowledgement	I have overall, good emotional, mental, and physical health
My daily life is a source of pleasure	I demonstrate care and concern in conversation, and I am good at considering others' perspectives	I am able to say "no" to people without feeling guilty	I can let go of self-defeating thoughts
I can manage stress well	I avoid unnecessary and unrealistic burdens and responsibilities	I determine if help is wanted or beneficial before attempting to help	I take time to be alone

UNDERSTAND AND TRANSFORM ANGER

Anger is a natural emotion, in response to something you either think should not have happened or something you think should have happened that did not happen. I call anger a response to a real or perceived injustice. Regardless, anger is not something you can avoid; you learn to understand it and you learn what to do with it. Try the exercise below: **e.g.**, when I feel: <u>angry, frustrated, and disappointed;</u> I then become <u>anxious, yell, shut down, and hold a grudge.</u>

When I feel ____
I then (what do you do)?

____

____

____

When I feel ____
I then (what do you do)?

____

____

____

When I feel ____
I then (what do you do)?

____

____

____

When I feel ____
I then (what do you do)?

____

____

____

When I feel ____

I then (what do you do)?

____

____

____

Now that you have identified the impact your feelings have on your behavior; you can work on changing what you are telling yourself about certain situations that lead to self-defeating emotions and behaviors that follow. Remember, with this book in your hand; you are holding the key to recovering your life. Your wait is over. You will no longer sit by and allow life situations, people, and even your own thought processes to keep you on the sidelines of life. You are playing to win, and win is what you will do.

ACTIVITY 6

DESIGN AND BUILD!!!

When building a house, there are times some people might ask a designer for help in creating the perfect image of their house. Input sought and needed in the process, varies from person-to-person. Now imagine that the house in this exercise represents your life. In designing and building the life you desire, you might seek help from a trusted friend, family member, professional, or spiritual advisor to help you with sculpting the life you want to live in.

The way to make the most of others' input is to first know yourself or possess healthy self-awareness to the degree that you are the ultimate decision-maker, as related to the final outcome or goal you desire. Since you will live in this house you are designing and building, you get to build it.

I am aware that, in your head, there are thoughts about what others want you to do, what you think you should do, must do, have to do, need to do, and ought to do. These demands can not only be crippling and stifling; but they can also limit your self-awareness and impede your creativity ability that is needed to live the life you can mostly enjoy.

In this exercise, you will consider what is needed in your life. How will you decorate your new life with healthy ways of thinking and healthy emotions? You will also decide on how you will cultivate healthy relationships in your new living space. Be gracious with yourself as you build. You might have limited resources to build, but it's okay. In time, you will develop tools and materials needed to have a satisfying life.

Examples of healthy thoughts….

Thoughts
Today is going to be a good day!
I enjoy many aspects of myself.

Being a healthy communicator is important to me.
Investing time in effective self-care adds more value to my life.
I desire to see others happy and healthy.
A bad moment does not mean my day will be bad, and a bad day does not mean my life is bad.
I have the ability to allow others to express their own perspective.
Variety in life is important to me.
Forgiveness is something I give; trust is something others must earn.

Now decide....

What tools do you currently possess (*in terms of thoughts, emotions, moods, and relationships*) that you will use to begin building. What tools do you need to eliminate (*in terms of thoughts, emotions, moods, and relationships*) that are not necessary, and what tools do you possess that you need to sharpen? Next to each response you write, place either a (**u**) for use (**e**) for eliminate (**s**) for sharpen.

<table>
<tr><td colspan="4" align="center">TOOLS</td></tr>
</table>

Thoughts	Emotions	Moods	Relationships

WHAT'S EATING YOU?

A common phrase you ask others, or others ask you is: What are you eating? Now I want to ask: what's eating you? When you are grumpy and tired, and can't seem to get things going mentally, emotionally, and physically, this is a good time to ask and answer this poignant question. You live a busy life, perhaps you are a parent and a spouse, or a single parent. Maybe you are in a stressful relationship and managing a very demanding career. Whatever your life dynamics are, you reach a place and time in your life that you feel as if something is eating away at you. Something is gnawing at your energy and your peace of mind. As if a parasite is within sucking the very life from you and draining you of all creativity and passion you would otherwise experience.

Try as you might, you cannot be all things to all people. You cannot build the life you desire and recover aspects of yourself that you have put to the side, if you do not take time to notice what the heck is going on with you. There are only a certain number of hours in the day. If you get adequate sleep of approximately seven to eight hours of a day; and you work, at minimum, eight hours per day that's fifteen to sixteen hours gone. You do not have very many awake hours left. Now do you understand why you are so super stressed?

Take a look at the following self-care strategies below. Circle all that are true for you, place an (X) next to any strategies that do not apply:

SELF-CARE

- Good sleep hygiene (at least 7 to 8 hours of sleep per night).
- Some form of exercise at least 3 times per week.
- Take at least a 15-minute powernap on days off and during work days when possible.
- Eat nutritiously at least 5 days per week.

- Get a good belly laugh at least once per day.

- Engage in meaningful conversation at least once per day, that does not include work.

- Engage in an activity by yourself.

- Get a massage, foot, or back rub.

- Refrain from putting demands on yourself such as I should, must, ought, have to and need to.

- Set healthy boundaries.

- Live a balanced life of work and fun.

- Can be assertive, versus passive and aggressive, when you express your wants, needs, and desires.

- Speak positive affirmations to yourself daily.

- Drink water daily.

- Take a lunch break at work, and you do not continue working while eating your lunch.

- Practice mindfulness daily.

- Give at least one person a compliment each day.

- Engage in self-awareness and learn something new about yourself at least once per week.

- Share good quality time with significant other or spouse at least once per day.

- Enjoy the company of friends at least once or twice per month.

Below, add strategies you engage in that were not mentioned, and strategies that you do not engage in that you would like to begin engaging in:

The more you are able to live a well-rounded life the better you can feel. Then you can realize even more that you are on your way to a life you can enjoy!

Activity 8

UNSCRAMBLE YOUR STRESS

How much do you know about stress? Do you know that good and bad stress elicits the same biological response? Whether you experience good stress associated with a new job, a new relationship, or the birth of a baby; or bad stress associated with loss, betrayal, or some other unfavorable situations. Your body goes through the same response. The following are a few examples of what you can expect to experience during stress:

- Sleep difficulties

- Headaches

- Muscle tension

- Fatigue

- Difficulty winding down

- Becoming jittery

- Inability to focus and concentrate

- Changes in appetite

EXERCISE

Unscramble the following words. When you are done, you will formulate coherent thoughts to create helpful ideas about stress management. (**if you become stuck, answers are in the back of the book**).

- pede   reathbgni   eveslrei   sertss

- lmels   werslfo   nda   lbow   ublesbb

- xaelr   rste   dna   leasere

- ngchae   nhitnkgi   ngecha   otnoisme cereasde sersts

- velodep   thlyeah   oosthign-fles

- setr   lelw

- pleimtemn   xciesere

- tainmain   thlyeah   shipslareiont

- notd   ssupreer   ouyrfles

- auglh   tofne

WHAT DO YOU KNOW ABOUT PROBLEM-SOLVING?

Your ask your co-worker a question and she is snippy with you; this is not the first time she has done this. How do you respond?

a. Snap back

b. Go to other co-workers and tell them to watch out for her

c. Do nothing

d. When she appears calm, ask if the two of you can talk in private and express concerns

e. Tell the supervisor about her behavior if talking privately is not effective

f. Both (d) and (e)

You are doing your best to implement strategies you have learned in this workbook. Your spouse/partner is not the best at communicating and this is becoming an irritant for you. You attempt to talk with him and he yells at you, walks away, and slams the bedroom door. What can be a helpful, healthy response?

    a. Be understanding and try to talk it over another time
    b. Suggest to him that you both need couples therapy
    c. Tell him to get anger management or you will divorce him
    d. Sit quietly and cry
    e. Give him space and hold a grudge
    f. Both (a) and (b)

Your best friend stops talking to you all of a sudden. She does not answer your calls or text messages. You attempt to reach out on social media and can see she is reading your messages, but not responding. Then she blocks you. You have no idea what is going on and she won't communicate. What is the best course of action to demonstrate you are improving in problem-solving?

    a. Just forget about her
    b. Go to her house and ask what is going on
    c. Try sending an email
    d. Give her space and hopefully she will eventually talk about it
    e. Pray for an opportunity for her to reach out to you so you can ignore her
    f. None of the above

Your adolescent child is being defiant and disrespectful. This is new behavior. You attempt to talk to your child after school today; he yells and says he hates you. What do you do?

a. Say nothing
b. Yell back and tell your child you will not tolerate such behavior
c. Tell your child "I hate you too!"
d. Realize that behavior is the language of children when something is wrong
e. Do nothing
f. Cry and tell yourself you have failed as a parent

While the aim is to select answers that are helpful and healthy; whatever you choose can be helpful to understanding more about yourself. Then you can begin to work on ways to improve where you might demonstrate weakness in areas of problem-solving. In the back of this workbook are the best answers to choose for effective problem-solving.

ACTIVITY 10

NO LIMITS

I love telling this story. When my son was in high school his school counselor informed us, with great concern, that he would not be able to graduate with his class because he was short too many credits. This information was told to him at the end of his junior year. Looking into my son's eyes, I asked: "Would you feel bad if you do not graduate with your class?" He said yes. I scheduled a time to speak with the counselor.

During our meeting, I asked the counselor how many credits did my son need to graduate. I then asked her if there is any way he can graduate, even if he has to work hard to do it? I was sure to stress "Is there any way?" She could not think of a way. I asked: "What if he goes to night school and summer school to make up the missing credits, and maintain a full senior schedule?" She said, if he can do it he can earn the credits needed, but he would be under a lot of pressure. I said to her, all we want to know if there is a way.

Not only did he attend night school, summer school, and classes during the day; but he also held onto his part-time job. I had not seen him work as hard as he worked in three years, than I saw him work in one year. He put himself through a lot because he believed there were no limits.

What are some areas that you feel limited in? Are there certain people who speak more to limitations in your life than they speak to possibilities? Today is your day of freedom from fear of limitations. When you are faced with doubting or believing in yourself, ask the magic question just as I did; ask if there is any way? You might be surprised that things you considered as limitations are actually very real possibilities.

EXERCISE

Think about some things in your past and/or your current life that you considered as limitations. It might be an idea for a small business, a book you want to write, a relationship you want to pursue, a place you want to visit, returning to school to further your education, try for a promotion, etc. In the box below I want you to write all of your limiting thoughts:

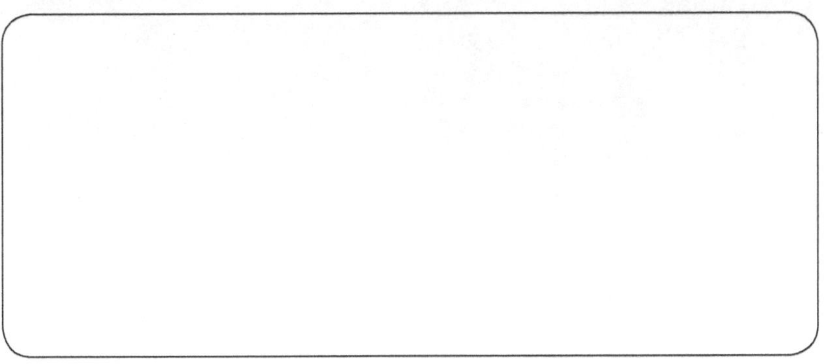

Now I want you to participate in a mental imagery of you putting those limitations in the shredder below:

Finally, write your new story below, including everything you left by the wayside when you allowed yourself to be limited by situations, people, and even limited by yourself.

YOUR NEW STORY!

Your Name Here: _______________________

ACTIVITY 11

CONTENTMENT DOES NOT MEAN COMPLACENT

You can be at a content place in your life, but this does not have to equal to complacency; and don't allow it to go there. Contentment is defined as being happy and satisfied. However, complacent is defined as showing smug satisfaction. Demonstrating self-approval to the degree that you are pleased or satisfied where you are. The danger in being complacent is that you fail to thrive and strive for more. I am not speaking of striving for more in a neurotic kind of way. When I speak of striving, I speak of the healthy aspect of human beings who continue to challenge themselves to learn, master, and achieve in a healthy manner; not driven by obsessive passion.

Are you content, but also seeking ways to grow and develop in a healthy manner, or are you complacent, reveling in the great things you have accomplished long, long ago; in a land far, far away; figuratively speaking? When you are content this means you are not putting pressure on yourself. When you are content, but not complacent; you realize that there is more to know, see, and do; things you have yet to experience.

In the following exercise you will write a letter to your past, present, and future self. You will talk to each of the phases of your life in terms of contentment and complacency; and each letter will include an exhortation.

e.g. (***dear past self***, I thank you for how you were there for me when I wanted to give up on my social life. I was afraid and I sat on the sidelines because I did not know what to do, I was so awkward and insecure. After a while I became content; but I also became complacent due to fear. You would not allow me to remain complacent, thank you!).

(***dear present self***, today when I was researching opportunities to enhance my skills on the job, I almost talked myself out of it because of the commitment I would need to make in order to move forward. Right now, my life is pretty easygoing and I don't know if I am ready to challenge myself; but you nudged me ever so gently and would not let me limit myself by being complacent, I'm grateful for you!).

(**_dear future self,_** thank you for hanging in there. There were times when your courage waned and your confidence took a nosedive; but you did not give up. Now just look at you; you are fierce and you are innovative. You brand yourself in many areas; you live out loud and you live passionately. I appreciate you!).

Now it's your turn...write:

____

____

____

____

____

____

____

____

____

____

____

____

____

ACTIVITY 12

DON'T LOOK BACK!

There are moments in life when looking back serves a purpose. These are the times when you look back on what you have learned, how far you have come over time, and how much you have grown and developed in your emotional intelligence and thinking. When you are looking back in regret, resentment, bitterness, and self-condemnation; you are doing your self a disservice.

TAKE A LOOK BACK...

I don't want you to look back too long. Maybe take a quick glance at first. Think of your driving experience. A rearview mirror is provided in vehicles for the purpose of being able to take a quick glance back while in motion. Learning to use your rearview mirror effectively is a part of being a good defensive driver. Think about it for a moment. What if you kept your gaze in your rearview mirror too long? You are correct; you would cause an accident. The same experience happens when we look too long into the past of our life.

This is not only true for looking back on experiences that might cause negative thoughts and emotions. This is also a true statement when looking back on positive experiences. When looking back too long on good, positive experiences you can begin to revel in the moments and lose focus on many more experiences and memories you can create. I have spoken to many people throughout my life, I can tell when they have stopped growing and developing by what they talk about mostly. Most of their conversations are about what they accomplished years ago, relationships they enjoyed in the past that might have ended through death, and memories of good days that they wish they could go back to.

I don't want you to get so caught up in what was or what has been, to the degree that you miss opportunities to realize what can be. In this exercise I want you to take a look back and scan your life experiences, choices, relationships, etc. You are in the driver seat of your life; imagine that you are looking back...

What do you see? Create a dedication statement to yourself as you look back. If there are moments you must grieve over and mourn the loss of, do so. Then I want you to thank your past experiences in life for all the lessons you have learned. Be grateful for the tough times, for they are the reason you are so strong and the reason you have not given up. By the time you end this statement, imagine yourself looking forward as you drive. Write a statement of exciting things to experience as you move forward and travel onward to new territory.

Looking back…

Looking ahead…

ONE MORE THING

Are you a "one more thing" kind of person? I used to be this kind of thinker. I would think there is always one more thing I could do to improve a relationship, or improve on a school project, or improve about myself. One day I realized that there will always be one more thing until I decide to think differently.

Try this exercise, in the square below I want you to write a situation and say this statement to yourself about the situation: "I know I gave it my all, but I could have done some things differently." Your situation could be about anything. For help on getting started, refer back to the examples I shared about certain situations I experienced.

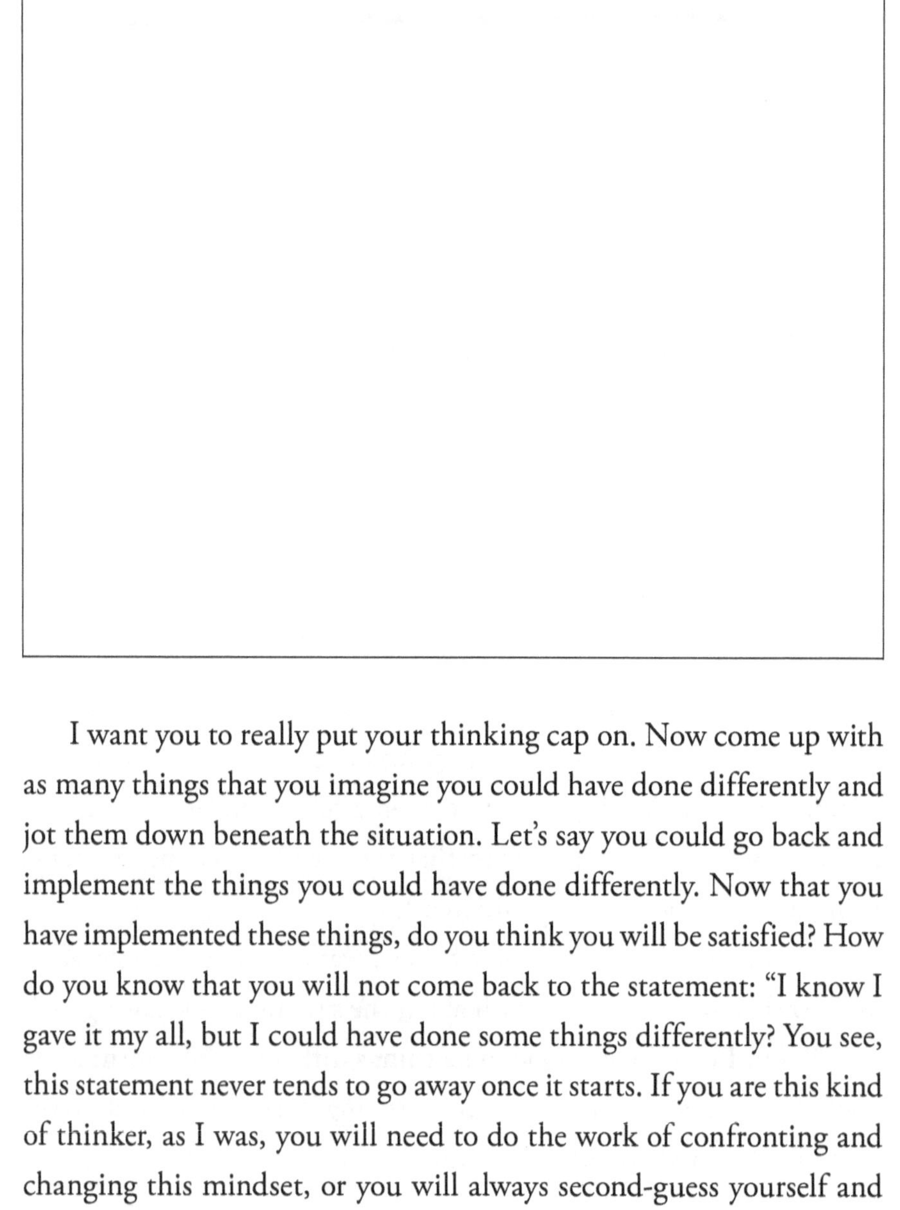

I want you to really put your thinking cap on. Now come up with as many things that you imagine you could have done differently and jot them down beneath the situation. Let's say you could go back and implement the things you could have done differently. Now that you have implemented these things, do you think you will be satisfied? How do you know that you will not come back to the statement: "I know I gave it my all, but I could have done some things differently? You see, this statement never tends to go away once it starts. If you are this kind of thinker, as I was, you will need to do the work of confronting and changing this mindset, or you will always second-guess yourself and remain on a neurotic hamster wheel. The next activity will be helpful for you to continue on your road of self-discovery and life recovery as you come to clear and healthy terms about what "good enough" is.

WHAT IS GOOD ENOUGH?

Regardless of what you have been told, or how you have been treated; regardless of what you have told yourself, or how you have treated yourself: you are good enough. Today is the day you learn to separate what you do from who you essentially are.

In order for you to quell negative thoughts and emotions you experience you must change your thinking. Open your mind to new ways of understanding yourself. I know you have learned to think a certain way over the years, but when you are ready to change you get to work.

You are engaging in this reading material because you want to know how to transform your thinking. You begin by taking in new information and deciding on whether or not you will allow a different commentary about you. Sure, there was a time that you believed what you were told, but today is a different day. Today you are in the driver's seat of your own life and you get to choose.

The road you take makes the difference. If you remain on the road of unhealthy stifling relationships you will always end up doubting your worth. You will need to surround yourself with positive people and environments that build you up and not tear you down. It is not easy to rebuild your life when you have questioned whether or not you are good enough for such a long time. But you will never accomplish anything different until you begin to do something different.

Give thought to the following questions and provide your answers. Reflect and meditate on your responses and continue to mull them over as you implement new ways of defining good enough.

1. What is your definition of "good enough?"

____

____

____

2. Who taught you to think of "good enough" in this way?

____

____

____

3. How has it been emotionally and mentally helpful in your life to think about "good enough" the way that you do?

____

____

____

4. How has it been emotionally and mentally harmful in your life to think about "good enough" the way that you do?

____

____

____

5. If you have been harmed by a certain way of thinking about what it means to be "good enough," what would be reasons to continue?

____

____

____

6. Do you give yourself permission to change your definition of "good enough?" If so, what will be your new definition and why?

____

____

____

Remember, whatever you call good enough, then stick by it. Don't be a wishy-washy thinker. Be firm in what you deem good enough and make an agreement with yourself that you, and only you get to decide what good enough means to you. If others get to decide what good enough is, why not you?

THE PERFECT RECIPE

You have learned a lot so far. You have covered good ground on your road to self-discovery and life recovery; but you still have much more ground to cover. In fact, self-discovery is a never-ending story. You continue to learn more and more about life and about yourself for as long as you live.

Everyone is different and we all need different things to function in a healthy manner, that creates life satisfaction. Because this is so, be sure not to compare yourself, your needs, your status in life, your choices, your relationships, your family, etc. You will do well to craft the perfect recipe for your life. You are a multifaceted individual; for sure there will be much variety to the ingredients that make a rich and satisfying life for you. I'll get you started on some examples: a recipe for a peaceful life experience could include relaxing in a spa, a massage, a walk on the beach or in the park, a kick-back with family and friends, a warm bath or shower, a good book by a cozy fireplace, a heart-warming movie, etc.

A recipe for a spontaneous and an exciting life experience could be a rollercoaster ride, skydiving, going to the airport without luggage or a plane ticket and randomly picking a place to travel, speed dating, etc. A recipe for an intellectually stimulating life experience could be joining a book club, going back to school, visits to the library, studying abroad, meetup groups for intellectuals, etc. NOW HAVE FUN FILLING THIS POT WITH YOUR PERFECT RECIPES!

Recipes

ACTIVITY 16

IN THE DARK

Anything in the dark grows. This is a good thing when a seed is in the darkness of a soil experience. However, when you keep things hidden in your life that you need to deal with in order to feel better, the dark does not serve you well. Also, the dark does not serve you well when you need to see how to get around in life and maneuver.

Have you ever piddled around in the dark and stubbed your toe or hit your head on a wall or door? I know I sure have. The dark is no fun when you need to get things done and you cannot see. Another bit of information about the dark, the longer you spend time in the dark the more you adjust. This is not something you want to do. Try this experiment. Try being in complete darkness at home. At first you will stumble around. But eventually you begin to use other senses to maneuver.

You engage your touch senses and move from place to place feeling your way around. Then you might notice you can hear a little better because you begin to use your senses that are accessible, since your vision cannot guide you. Pretty soon, you might notice you have become a little more comfortable in the dark. Now let's turn your attention to darkness as a representative of a lack of awareness.

When you are in the dark about a matter or about pertinent things in life that you need for personal growth and development, you are at a deficit. Be sure that you make every effort to turn the light on every dark situation that is important to your goals for self-discovery and life recovery. What have you been hiding in the dark that you are afraid to face? Go to the journal section of this workbook and create an entry. If there is someone you need to confront or make amends, consider how this might be helpful to do in order for you to be effective on your road to self-discovery and life recovery.

A CRUMB, A SLICE, OR A LOAF

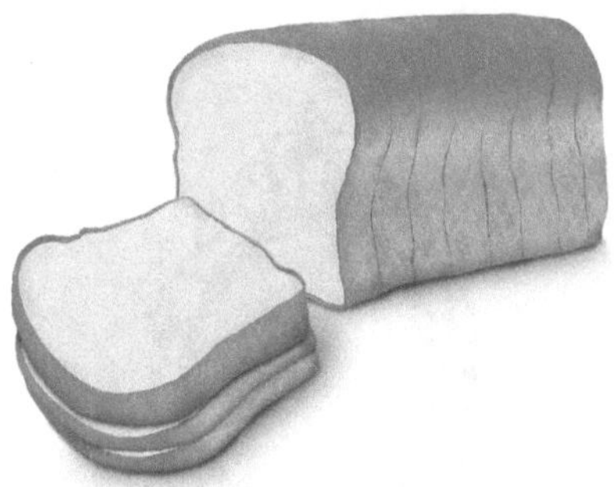

What do you want? As you reflect, can you recall experiences when you exerted a lot of energy, time, and effort for something or someone; and the results were not commensurate? This is what I call reaping results of a crumb or slice, instead of a loaf. As you grow on your road to the life you desire, be sure that you go after the loaf. Why work hard and with intensity for a crumb or a slice, when you can have the entire loaf. Do not settle for anything less than the best that you pour into your goals.

Don't allow others to dummy down what you deserve. You have lived too long going after crumbs, and accepting a slice here and there. Today is the day to have the whole loaf. Why not? The ingredients are the same so go for more of what you have been accepting and settling for all along. Do you recall other activities discussed earlier when you were encouraged to cultivate healthy relationships? You will also do well to seek out healthy environments in which you can grow, and then you can soar. Like an eagle you will soar high and seek after greater knowledge and experiences. You will thrive and strive to allow your great essence to glow.

EXERCISE…

Take a look into the mirror. What do you see as you look back at yourself? What is the message you are receiving from your inner critic that keeps you settling for less? How prepared are you to combat the negative narrative you have heard from others and perhaps you have spoken to yourself? Write your thoughts below:

____

Journal Prompts

You might need a little help with getting started on your journal writing journey, so I have added a few prompts to get you started; consider the following:

- I can love again...
- As a child, my most intimidating and fearful time was...
- Thoughts about being treated differently...
- How did I learn to limit myself?...
- Pain can only hurt if I allow...
- When did my anger start?...
- When I look at the way I behave, I see my mother, father, siblings, ex, etc.
- Why am I so hard on myself, but I am patient with others?...
- Why do people think I am mean?...
- My insecurities include...
- I no longer want to feel this low...
- Why did_____________________________ hurt me?...

- How do I learn to forgive_________________________ for doing_____________________?...
- I think I have low self-esteem because…
- Today can be a good day if I…
- I am good enough…

Moments Matter
6-Month Journal

________________________ , 20 ____

TO

________________________ , 20 ____

Date: _____________, 20___

MOMENTS MATTER

Date: _____________, 20___

MOMENTS MATTER

Date: ______________, 20____

MOMENTS MATTER

____
____
____
____
____
____
____
____
____
____
____
____
____
____
____
____

Date: ______________, 20____

MOMENTS MATTER

____
____
____
____
____
____
____
____
____
____
____
____
____
____
____
____

Date: _______________, 20____

MOMENTS MATTER

____

____

____

____

____

____

____

____

____

____

____

____

____

____

____

____

Date: _______________, 20____

MOMENTS MATTER

____

____

____

____

____

____

____

____

____

____

____

____

____

____

____

____

Date: _____________, 20____

MOMENTS MATTER

____
____
____
____
____
____
____
____
____
____
____
____
____
____
____

Date: _____________, 20____

MOMENTS MATTER

____
____
____
____
____
____
____
____
____
____
____
____
____
____
____
____

Date: _______________, 20____

Moments Matter

____
____
____
____
____
____
____
____
____
____
____
____
____
____
____
____

Date: _______________, 20____

Moments Matter

____
____
____
____
____
____
____
____
____
____
____
____
____
____
____
____

Date: _____________, 20____

MOMENTS MATTER

____
____
____
____
____
____
____
____
____
____
____
____
____
____
____

Date: _____________, 20____

MOMENTS MATTER

____
____
____
____
____
____
____
____
____
____
____
____
____
____
____

Date: ______________, 20____

MOMENTS MATTER

____

____

____

____

____

____

____

____

____

____

____

____

____

____

Date: ______________, 20____

MOMENTS MATTER

____

____

____

____

____

____

____

____

____

____

____

____

____

____

Date: _____________, 20___

MOMENTS MATTER

____
____
____
____
____
____
____
____
____
____
____
____
____

Date: _____________, 20___

MOMENTS MATTER

____
____
____
____
____
____
____
____
____
____
____
____
____
____
____
____
____
____

Date: _____________, 20____

MOMENTS MATTER

Date: _____________, 20____

MOMENTS MATTER

Date: _____________, 20___

MOMENTS MATTER

____

____

____

____

____

____

____

____

____

____

____

____

____

____

Date: _____________, 20___

MOMENTS MATTER

____

____

____

____

____

____

____

____

____

____

____

____

____

____

____

Date: _______________, 20____

Moments Matter

____
____
____
____
____
____
____
____
____
____
____
____
____
____
____
____

Date: _______________, 20____

Moments Matter

____
____
____
____
____
____
____
____
____
____
____
____
____
____
____
____

Date: _____________, 20___

MOMENTS MATTER

____
____
____
____
____
____
____
____
____
____
____
____
____
____

Date: _____________, 20___

MOMENTS MATTER

____
____
____
____
____
____
____
____
____
____
____
____
____
____

Date: _______________, 20___

MOMENTS MATTER

Date: _______________, 20___

MOMENTS MATTER

Date: _____________, 20____

Moments Matter

____
____
____
____
____
____
____
____
____
____
____
____
____
____
____
____

Date: _____________, 20____

Moments Matter

____
____
____
____
____
____
____
____
____
____
____
____
____
____
____
____
____
____
____
____

Date: ________________, 20____

MOMENTS MATTER

____

____

____

____

____

____

____

____

____

____

____

____

____

____

____

____

____

____

Date: ________________, 20____

MOMENTS MATTER

____

____

____

____

____

____

____

____

____

____

____

____

____

____

____

____

____

____

Date: _____________, 20___

MOMENTS MATTER

____
____
____
____
____
____
____
____
____
____
____
____
____
____

Date: _____________, 20___

MOMENTS MATTER

____
____
____
____
____
____
____
____
____
____
____
____
____
____

Date: _____________, 20____

MOMENTS MATTER

____
____
____
____
____
____
____
____
____
____
____
____
____
____
____
____
____
____

Date: _____________, 20____

MOMENTS MATTER

____
____
____
____
____
____
____
____
____
____
____
____
____
____
____
____
____

Date: _______________, 20____

MOMENTS MATTER

____
____
____
____
____
____
____
____
____
____
____
____
____
____

Date: _______________, 20____

MOMENTS MATTER

____
____
____
____
____
____
____
____
____
____
____
____
____
____
____
____

Date: _______________, 20___

MOMENTS MATTER

____
____
____
____
____
____
____
____
____
____
____
____
____
____
____

Date: _______________, 20___

MOMENTS MATTER

____
____
____
____
____
____
____
____
____
____
____
____
____
____
____

Date: ____________, 20___

MOMENTS MATTER

Date: ____________, 20___

MOMENTS MATTER

Date: _____________, 20____

MOMENTS MATTER

____
____
____
____
____
____
____
____
____
____
____
____
____
____
____
____

Date: _____________, 20____

MOMENTS MATTER

____
____
____
____
____
____
____
____
____
____
____
____
____
____
____
____

Date: _____________, 20___

MOMENTS MATTER

Date: _____________, 20___

MOMENTS MATTER

Date: _____________, 20____

MOMENTS MATTER

____
____
____
____
____
____
____
____
____
____
____
____
____
____
____
____
____

Date: _____________, 20____

MOMENTS MATTER

____
____
____
____
____
____
____
____
____
____
____
____
____
____
____
____
____

Date: _____________, 20___

MOMENTS MATTER

Date: _____________, 20___

MOMENTS MATTER

Date: ______________, 20___

MOMENTS MATTER

Date: ______________, 20___

MOMENTS MATTER

Date: _____________, 20____

MOMENTS MATTER

____
____
____
____
____
____
____
____
____
____
____
____
____

Date: _____________, 20____

MOMENTS MATTER

____
____
____
____
____
____
____
____
____
____
____
____
____
____
____

Date: ______________, 20____

MOMENTS MATTER

____

____

____

____

____

____

____

____

____

____

____

____

____

____

____

____

Date: ______________, 20____

MOMENTS MATTER

____

____

____

____

____

____

____

____

____

____

____

____

____

____

____

____

Date: ________________, 20____

MOMENTS MATTER

Date: ________________, 20____

MOMENTS MATTER

Date: ____________, 20___

MOMENTS MATTER

Date: ____________, 20___

MOMENTS MATTER

Date: _____________, 20____

MOMENTS MATTER

____
____
____
____
____
____
____
____
____
____
____
____
____
____

Date: _____________, 20____

MOMENTS MATTER

____
____
____
____
____
____
____
____
____
____
____
____
____
____

Date: ______________, 20___

MOMENTS MATTER

Date: ______________, 20___

MOMENTS MATTER

Date: _____________, 20____

MOMENTS MATTER

____

____

____

____

____

____

____

____

____

____

____

____

____

____

____

Date: _____________, 20____

MOMENTS MATTER

____

____

____

____

____

____

____

____

____

____

____

____

____

____

____

Date: _______________, 20____

Moments Matter

____
____
____
____
____
____
____
____
____
____
____
____
____
____

Date: _______________, 20____

Moments Matter

____
____
____
____
____
____
____
____
____
____
____
____
____
____

Date: _____________, 20____

MOMENTS MATTER

____
____
____
____
____
____
____
____
____
____
____
____
____
____
____

Date: _____________, 20____

MOMENTS MATTER

____
____
____
____
____
____
____
____
____
____
____
____
____
____
____
____
____

Date: ______________, 20____

MOMENTS MATTER

____
____
____
____
____
____
____
____
____
____
____
____
____
____
____
____

Date: ______________, 20____

MOMENTS MATTER

____
____
____
____
____
____
____
____
____
____
____
____
____
____
____
____

Date: _____________, 20____

MOMENTS MATTER

Date: _____________, 20____

MOMENTS MATTER

Date: _______________, 20___

MOMENTS MATTER

____

____

____

____

____

____

____

____

____

____

____

____

____

____

Date: _______________, 20___

MOMENTS MATTER

____

____

____

____

____

____

____

____

____

____

____

____

____

____

Date: _____________, 20____

MOMENTS MATTER

____
____
____
____
____
____
____
____
____
____
____
____
____
____
____
____

Date: _____________, 20____

MOMENTS MATTER

____
____
____
____
____
____
____
____
____
____
____
____
____
____
____
____

Date: _____________, 20___

MOMENTS MATTER

____
____
____
____
____
____
____
____
____
____
____
____
____
____
____
____

Date: _____________, 20___

MOMENTS MATTER

____
____
____
____
____
____
____
____
____
____
____
____
____
____
____
____

Date: _______________, 20____

MOMENTS MATTER

____
____
____
____
____
____
____
____
____
____
____
____
____
____

Date: _______________, 20____

MOMENTS MATTER

____
____
____
____
____
____
____
____
____
____
____
____
____
____
____
____
____
____

Date: _______________, 20____

MOMENTS MATTER

Date: _______________, 20____

MOMENTS MATTER

Date: _______________, 20___

MOMENTS MATTER

Date: _______________, 20___

MOMENTS MATTER

Date: _____________, 20___

MOMENTS MATTER

____

Date: _____________, 20___

MOMENTS MATTER

____

Date: ______________, 20___

MOMENTS MATTER

____
____
____
____
____
____
____
____
____
____
____
____
____

Date: ______________, 20___

MOMENTS MATTER

____
____
____
____
____
____
____
____
____
____
____
____
____
____
____

Date: _____________, 20____

MOMENTS MATTER

____
____
____
____
____
____
____
____
____
____
____
____
____
____
____
____

Date: _____________, 20____

MOMENTS MATTER

____
____
____
____
____
____
____
____
____
____
____
____
____
____
____
____

Date: _____________, 20___

MOMENTS MATTER

____
____
____
____
____
____
____
____
____
____
____
____
____
____
____

Date: _____________, 20___

MOMENTS MATTER

____
____
____
____
____
____
____
____
____
____
____
____
____
____
____
____

Date: _______________, 20____

MOMENTS MATTER

____
____
____
____
____
____
____
____
____
____
____
____
____
____
____
____
____

Date: _______________, 20____

MOMENTS MATTER

____
____
____
____
____
____
____
____
____
____
____
____
____
____
____
____
____

Date: _____________, 20___

MOMENTS MATTER

Date: _____________, 20___

MOMENTS MATTER

Date: _____________, 20___

MOMENTS MATTER

____
____
____
____
____
____
____
____
____
____
____
____
____
____
____

Date: _____________, 20___

MOMENTS MATTER

____
____
____
____
____
____
____
____
____
____
____
____
____
____
____

Date: _______________, 20____

MOMENTS MATTER

Date: _______________, 20____

MOMENTS MATTER

Date: _______________, 20____

Moments Matter

____
____
____
____
____
____
____
____
____
____
____
____
____
____
____

Date: _______________, 20____

Moments Matter

____
____
____
____
____
____
____
____
____
____
____
____
____
____
____

Date: _______________, 20___

MOMENTS MATTER

____
____
____
____
____
____
____
____
____
____
____
____
____
____

Date: _______________, 20___

MOMENTS MATTER

____
____
____
____
____
____
____
____
____
____
____
____
____
____
____
____

Date: _____________, 20___

MOMENTS MATTER

____
____
____
____
____
____
____
____
____
____
____
____
____
____
____

Date: _____________, 20___

MOMENTS MATTER

____
____
____
____
____
____
____
____
____
____
____
____
____
____
____

Date: _______________, 20____

MOMENTS MATTER

____
____
____
____
____
____
____
____
____
____
____
____
____
____
____

Date: _______________, 20____

MOMENTS MATTER

____
____
____
____
____
____
____
____
____
____
____
____
____
____
____
____
____

Date: _______________, 20___

Moments Matter

Date: _______________, 20___

Moments Matter

Date: ______________, 20___

MOMENTS MATTER

Date: ______________, 20___

MOMENTS MATTER

Date: ____________, 20___

Moments Matter

Date: ____________, 20___

Moments Matter

Date: _______________, 20____

Moments Matter

____
____
____
____
____
____
____
____
____
____
____
____
____
____
____

Date: _______________, 20____

Moments Matter

____
____
____
____
____
____
____
____
____
____
____
____
____
____
____
____

Date: _____________, 20___

MOMENTS MATTER

____
____
____
____
____
____
____
____
____
____
____
____
____
____

Date: _____________, 20___

MOMENTS MATTER

____
____
____
____
____
____
____
____
____
____
____
____
____
____

Date: _______________, 20____

MOMENTS MATTER

____
____
____
____
____
____
____
____
____
____
____
____
____
____

Date: _______________, 20____

MOMENTS MATTER

____
____
____
____
____
____
____
____
____
____
____
____
____
____

Date: _____________, 20___

MOMENTS MATTER

____

Date: _____________, 20___

MOMENTS MATTER

____

Date: _______________, 20____

MOMENTS MATTER

____
____
____
____
____
____
____
____
____
____
____
____
____
____
____

Date: _______________, 20____

MOMENTS MATTER

____
____
____
____
____
____
____
____
____
____
____
____
____
____
____
____
____

Date: _______________, 20____

MOMENTS MATTER

____

____

____

____

____

____

____

____

____

____

____

____

____

Date: _______________, 20____

MOMENTS MATTER

____

____

____

____

____

____

____

____

____

____

____

____

____

Date: _______________, 20____

Moments Matter

____

____

____

____

____

____

____

____

____

____

____

____

____

Date: _______________, 20____

Moments Matter

____

____

____

____

____

____

____

____

____

____

____

____

____

Date: _______________, 20____

MOMENTS MATTER

Date: _______________, 20____

MOMENTS MATTER

Date: _____________, 20____

MOMENTS MATTER

____
____
____
____
____
____
____
____
____
____
____
____
____
____

Date: _____________, 20____

MOMENTS MATTER

____
____
____
____
____
____
____
____
____
____
____
____
____
____
____
____

Date: _______________, 20____

MOMENTS MATTER

Date: _______________, 20____

MOMENTS MATTER

Moments Matter

Date: ___________, 20___

____
____
____
____
____
____
____
____
____
____
____
____
____
____

Moments Matter

Date: ___________, 20___

____
____
____
____
____
____
____
____
____
____
____
____
____
____
____
____
____

Date: _______________, 20___

MOMENTS MATTER

____
____
____
____
____
____
____
____
____
____
____
____
____
____
____
____
____

Date: _______________, 20___

MOMENTS MATTER

____
____
____
____
____
____
____
____
____
____
____
____
____
____
____
____
____
____

Date: _____________, 20____

MOMENTS MATTER

____
____
____
____
____
____
____
____
____
____
____
____
____
____

Date: _____________, 20____

MOMENTS MATTER

____
____
____
____
____
____
____
____
____
____
____
____
____
____
____
____

Date: _______________, 20____

MOMENTS MATTER

____
____
____
____
____
____
____
____
____
____
____
____
____
____
____
____
____

Date: _______________, 20____

MOMENTS MATTER

____
____
____
____
____
____
____
____
____
____
____
____
____
____
____
____
____

Date: _______________, 20___

MOMENTS MATTER

____
____
____
____
____
____
____
____
____
____
____
____
____
____

Date: _______________, 20___

MOMENTS MATTER

____
____
____
____
____
____
____
____
____
____
____
____
____
____

Date: _____________, 20___

MOMENTS MATTER

____
____
____
____
____
____
____
____
____
____
____
____
____
____
____
____

Date: _____________, 20___

MOMENTS MATTER

____
____
____
____
____
____
____
____
____
____
____
____
____
____
____
____

Date: ______________, 20____

MOMENTS MATTER

____
____
____
____
____
____
____
____
____
____
____
____
____
____
____

Date: ______________, 20____

MOMENTS MATTER

____
____
____
____
____
____
____
____
____
____
____
____
____
____
____
____

Date: ______________, 20____

MOMENTS MATTER

____
____
____
____
____
____
____
____
____
____
____
____
____
____
____

Date: ______________, 20____

MOMENTS MATTER

____
____
____
____
____
____
____
____
____
____
____
____
____
____
____

Date: ______________, 20___

MOMENTS MATTER

____

____

____

____

____

____

____

____

____

____

____

____

____

____

Date: ______________, 20___

MOMENTS MATTER

____

____

____

____

____

____

____

____

____

____

____

____

____

____

____

Date: _____________, 20___

MOMENTS MATTER

____
____
____
____
____
____
____
____
____
____
____
____
____
____
____
____

Date: _____________, 20___

MOMENTS MATTER

____
____
____
____
____
____
____
____
____
____
____
____
____
____
____
____

Date: _____________, 20___

MOMENTS MATTER

____

____

____

____

____

____

____

____

____

____

____

____

____

____

Date: _____________, 20___

MOMENTS MATTER

____

____

____

____

____

____

____

____

____

____

____

____

____

____

____

____

Date: _______________, 20___

MOMENTS MATTER

____
____
____
____
____
____
____
____
____
____
____
____
____

Date: _______________, 20___

MOMENTS MATTER

____
____
____
____
____
____
____
____
____
____
____
____
____
____

Date: _____________, 20____

MOMENTS MATTER

____
____
____
____
____
____
____
____
____
____
____
____
____

Date: _____________, 20____

MOMENTS MATTER

____
____
____
____
____
____
____
____
____
____
____
____
____

Date: _______________, 20____

MOMENTS MATTER

____
____
____
____
____
____
____
____
____
____
____
____
____
____
____
____
____

Date: _______________, 20____

MOMENTS MATTER

____
____
____
____
____
____
____
____
____
____
____
____
____
____
____
____
____

Date: ________________, 20____

MOMENTS MATTER

____
____
____
____
____
____
____
____
____
____
____
____
____
____

Date: ________________, 20____

MOMENTS MATTER

____
____
____
____
____
____
____
____
____
____
____
____
____
____
____
____
____
____

Date: _____________, 20____

MOMENTS MATTER

____

____

____

____

____

____

____

____

____

____

____

____

____

____

____

____

____

Date: _____________, 20____

MOMENTS MATTER

____

____

____

____

____

____

____

____

____

____

____

____

____

____

____

____

____

Date: ______________, 20____

MOMENTS MATTER

Date: ______________, 20____

MOMENTS MATTER

Date: _____________, 20___

MOMENTS MATTER

Date: _____________, 20___

MOMENTS MATTER

Date: _____________, 20____

MOMENTS MATTER

____
____
____
____
____
____
____
____
____
____
____
____
____
____

Date: _____________, 20____

MOMENTS MATTER

____
____
____
____
____
____
____
____
____
____
____
____
____
____
____

Date: _____________, 20____

MOMENTS MATTER

Date: _____________, 20____

MOMENTS MATTER

Date: _______________, 20____

MOMENTS MATTER

____

____

____

____

Date: _______________, 20____

MOMENTS MATTER

____

____

____

____

Date: _____________, 20____

MOMENTS MATTER

____
____
____
____
____
____
____
____
____
____
____
____
____
____
____
____
____
____

Date: _____________, 20____

MOMENTS MATTER

____
____
____
____
____
____
____
____
____
____
____
____
____
____
____
____
____
____

Date: _______________, 20____

MOMENTS MATTER

____
____
____
____
____
____
____
____
____
____
____
____
____
____
____

Date: _______________, 20____

MOMENTS MATTER

____
____
____
____
____
____
____
____
____
____
____
____
____
____
____

Date: _____________, 20___

MOMENTS MATTER

____
____
____
____
____
____
____
____
____
____
____
____
____

Date: _____________, 20___

MOMENTS MATTER

____
____
____
____
____
____
____
____
____
____
____
____
____
____
____

Date: ____________, 20___

MOMENTS MATTER

____
____
____

Date: ____________, 20___

MOMENTS MATTER

____
____
____

Date: ______________, 20____

Moments Matter

____
____
____
____
____
____
____
____
____
____
____
____
____
____
____
____
____
____

Date: ______________, 20____

Moments Matter

____
____
____
____
____
____
____
____
____
____
____
____
____
____
____
____
____
____

Activity 8 answers

1. deep breathing relieves stress
2. smell flowers and blow bubbles
3. relax rest and release
4. change thinking change emotions decrease stress
5. develop healthy self-soothing
6. rest well
7. laugh often
8. implement exercise
9. maintain healthy relationships
10. don't pressure yourself

Activity 9 answers

1. f
2. f
3. d
4. d

About the Author

Crystal Scott is a Licensed Marriage and Family Therapist in the states of California, Texas, and Michigan. She holds a Master's Degree in Counseling Psychology as well as a certificate in Pastoral Counseling from Holy Names University, Oakland, CA. Crystal graduated Magna cum Laude with a Bachelor's of Science Degree in Organizational Management from Patten University, Oakland CA. Her primary private practice location is in the DFW Texas Region, which she established over 7 years ago after relocating from the California, San Francisco Bay Area. Crystal opened her second private practice location in Detroit Michigan 4 years ago. She has been in her role as therapist for approximately 17 years. Her credentials afford her opportunities to provide critical incident and stress debriefing (CISD) services to many organizations and employment companies. Crystal also facilitates teaching and training on various topics for mental health, coping, and employee assistance needs. Additionally, Crystal is the author of *Take Back Your Life, Sin and the Church, Communication and You, How Can I Laugh,* and *Unstoppable: Passion Unleashed.*

Connect with Crystal

@ cmscott_therapist on Instagram

@cmscounseling1 on Twitter

@ N'DA MIX WITH CRISSY on YouTube

@https://ndamix283423163.wordpress.com

EMAIL: cmscounseling1@gmail.com

WEBSITE: cmscott-lmft-therapist.com

Resources Include

Motivational speaking

Educational training for large and small businesses

Self-Improvement groups for all ages

Daily blogs

Premarital therapy (with certificate)

And much more....!